CITY OF ANGELS

The History of Recoleta Cemetery

A guide to its treasures

OMAR LOPEZ MATO

Auspiciado por:
Sponsored by:
"Secretaría de Cultura y Medios de Comunicación de la Presidencia de la Nación".
(Media and Cultural Secretariat of the Nation).
"Secretaría de Cultura del Gobierno de la Ciudad Autónoma de Buenos Aires".
(Cultural Secretariat of the city of Buenos Aires).

Publishing Direction
   Omar López Mato

General Coordination
   Omar López Mato
   Daniel Villarroel

Translator
   Eva Iaconis Cabral

Corrector
   Paula Judith Mitar

Art Direction
   Gráfica Integral S.A.

Printing and bound
   Gráfica Integral S.A.
   Buenos Aires, Argentina.

Photography
   Omar López Mato

This book is an abridged edition of the Spanish version "Ciudad de Angeles" – **Historia del cementerio de la Recoleta.**

As in the previous edition I have to thank my crew: Matías Garabedián, Daniel Villarroel, Ignacio Jaeschke, Ezequiel Lopez Mato and Jorge Ruiz.

For the present book the assistance of Eva Iaconis Cabral for the translation and the ideas of Julia Ferramosca and Pablo Giannattasio from Gráfica Integral have proved to be of utmost importance.

And as for every aspect of my life, the presence of my son and daughters: Tamara, Ezequiel, Celina, Malena and Paula and the loving care and eternal patience of Mariana Sere, without which every effort is senseless.

CITY OF ANGELS

The History of Recoleta Cemetery

www.ciudaddeangeles.com

INTRODUCTION
How to use this book

This book does not only pretend to introduce you to the stories and artistic values of this cemetery, because of the importance of those buried here, but it also pretends to have a mere glimpse of the conflictive Argentine history.

So, as an introduction we try to summarize different moments of the national history, especially those events connected with the beautiful Pilar church and to its cemetery which stands over the ancient garden that the recoletos monks cultivated. Seized by the governor Martín Rodríguez and his minister, the future first President of the Nation, Bernardino Rivadavia, turned it into a necropoly in 1822, and for years was the only cemetery in town and elected place where the "well to do" citizens of Buenos Aires wished to stay for the rest of eternity.

So the wealthy people of a rich nation stood up to their pretended level copying castles, buildings and cemeteries from their voyages abroad, especially Europe, where they would stay for months and even years.

So these "princes" of the pampas copied the Italian and French bourgeoises not only in clothes and spirit but also in the sculptures they admired at Pere Lachaise in Paris and Stagnieto in Genoa.

The second part of the book, depicts and tells the personal events that preceded the most outstanding vaults. Each one (or group of vaults as we put together families) has its own photo and a petit map, so as to find it in this 10 acres cemetery.

We also detail a walking itinerary where we expand more general information. A number within brackets will show the page where a particular vault or family history is presented with more specifications.

Finally, a map with the most important mausoleums and vaults is shown on the last pages.

Hoping this book will help you to make this a memorable visit, we wish the best of lucks during your stay in our country, and specially this cemetery, pride of our Nation.

ARGENTINA
A brief history

I n order to have an approach for a better understanding of the importance that the Recoleta Cemetery has for the Argentinians, we must explore its history so the visitor will be able to grasp some of the feelings that this place arises.

Buenos Aires was founded twice. The first time by Pedro de Mendoza, the "Adelantado" (A Spanish word similar to "pioneer"). Unfortunately, his mission ended in a huge failure, paradoxically due to the hunger in a land that was once known as "The Barn of the World".

The second founder was Juan de Garay who had left from Asuncion del Paraguay and settled with only a few followers, dividing into parcels the city surroundings. The first owner of the place where the necropolis actually stands was Ortiz de Zárate, a Spanish knight descendant from an Inca princess. The life of the town at those times was simply miserable; just a few huts grew sluggishly with the settlers dreaming to leave all their pains behind.

But better times were about to come. The town turned wealthy, not just because of the immense amount of cattle grassing around, but for a very special industry: smuggling. Bribing the burocratic Spanish colonial economy was big business, thanks to the smugglering advantages it possessed: an easily reachable river, tunnels especially built, so nobody could watch the merchandise (these tunnels can be seen at the "Enlightment Square", at the downtown area) and the easily bribed governors, who participated in these misdemeanours and made huge fortunes in return. This was the time (1732) when the beautiful Pilar church was built in honour to the Virgin of Zaragoza. Every October 12th, the "romerias" (popular feasts) were celebrated around the church with music, dancing and horse racing, tradition that lasted until the beginning of the 20th century and still persists in discos and fashionable restaurants.

The city kept growing with splendor. In 1806, England (at that time in war with Spain) looked at Buenos Aires as a sparkling diamond for its crown and invaded it. It was easily conquered, due to the general surprise and the cowardly escape of the Viceroy Sobremonte. A recovery movement was started by a French born navy officer, Santiago de Liniers, who prayed at this church the day before he took command of the situation. Thanks to his gallant bravery, he was appointed Viceroy and became the leader of the defense during the second invasion in 1807. Few years later when the patriotic movement began, as he remained faithful to the Spanish crown, he was executed by his former followers.

During 1810 when the King of Spain, Fernando VII was held prisoner by Napoleon, our people thought that as there was no King there shouldn't be a Viceroy; consequently they felt free to choose their government. War broke against the Spanish who held strong at the north of the country. An army was led against them, commanded by a lawyer turned to general, Manuel Belgrano, who served for several years with triumphs and defeats, dying in extreme poverty and buried at the church of Santo Domingo where you can appreciate his beautiful mausoleum done by Ettore Ximenes. At that time, many officers serving for Spain but born in America, returned to Buenos Aires to offer their swords for the cause. Alvear, Estomba, Chilavert, Zapiola and the most important, Father of our Nation, the Liberator José Francisco de San Martín, who drew an army through the Andes (our gigantic mountain range) and granted the desired freedom to us, Chile and Peru, and help to drive the Spanish away from Latin America. His wife, Remedios de Escalada, was born and died in Buenos Aires. She was buried here, as well as her brothers, all National heroes. In 1825, San Martín turned in his command to Simón Bolívar and departed to France in ostracism where he died 25 years later, surrounded by his beloved daughter and granddaughters. His body was brought back to Argentina in 1885 and it is actually buried at the Cathedral in a beautiful Carrara tomb made by French artist Carrierre Beleusse.

Thus, the country was now in a state to declare its independence and so it did on July 9th, 1816 in the small town of Tucumán, under the influence of the Supreme Director Juan Martín de Pueyrredón, San Martín's friend and supporter.

But even though the country was free and independent and the threat of a Spanish invasion was vanishing, there was no general agreement upon the way the nation was to be governed.

Many constitutions were voted but none was put into practice. So, two main different positions developed. On one hand, most of the provinces wanted a federal government with each one having the necessary freedom to decide on its own convenience, while most of the people from Buenos Aires, called "porteños" (from port) – since this city was the main port of the country and the place where Customs collected most of the money – were reluctant to share their incomes with other towns. Their members promoted a united system (Unitarians, as they were known).

This dilema evolved into civil wars, which lasted – with some short peace periods – from 1820 to 1853. One of those relatively peaceful moments was during Gral. Martín Rodriguez' government (he is buried at the Recoleta cemetery with an excellent sculpture by Arturo Dresco) and the first President of Argentina, the progressive, but prematurely ahead of his time, Bernardino Rivadavia, to whom we owe the idea of creating this cemetery in 1822, forbidding to bury inside the churches, as it was the use from colonial times to that date. In spite of his efforts to keep the country updated to the new political ideas, his government was unpopular. Though a war was won against Brazil in 1828 for its invasion to Uruguay (at that time, part of the United Provinces) his management was badly harmed and Uruguay was hopelessly lost due to the disastrous diplomatic handling of the situation. Rivadavia had to run away staying in Europe until his death in Cadiz (Spain). He was brought back to the country, buried for some years at the cemetery he had promoted and finally placed into his monument at Plaza Once, a fantastic piece of work by the Argentinian sculptor José Yrurtia.
Then, a popular governor was elected: the hero of the independence, lately vanished to Baltimore-USA, Colonel Manuel Dorrego, leader of the Federal Party.

His policy was just opposite to Rivadavia's and created a quarrelsome climate among the intellectual elite that pressed over the disappointed young officers coming back from the Brazilian front. The most outstanding of them was the 30 year-old General Juan Galo Lavalle, who had not only fought the Brazilian war with courage and honour but also campaigned from Chile to Peru with San Martín and afterwards under Bolívar command, known as the "Lion of Riobamba" battle, where he defeated a Spanish regiment five times his force.

Lavalle drove Dorrego away and after defeating him at Navarro, ordered his execution under strong pressure of some Unitarian supporters, even though his friends and subordinates pleaded him mercy for his captive. This merciless bloodshed, was severely criticized and caused Lavalle to quit the government, staying in Uruguay where he rested in peace for 10 long years. But then, he was compelled to take command of an army against Juan Manuel de Rosas who had turned to be the strong man of the country. Rosas belonged to a wealthy land and cattle owner family. He had ruled his vast "estancias" with unquestionable authority and was not used to having or hearing any complain to his commands. In the same way, he managed the country as a huge ranch, not allowing any opposition and vanishing any possible disturbance, sometimes with unnecessary brutality. But he believed this was the only way to bring peace. Of course, those contrary to his position, not only intellectuals but also wealthy farmers, took advantage of a French siege to Buenos Aires in 1838 and asked the retired General Lavalle to drive an army against Rosas in the name of freedom.

Due to lack of organization and a short sighted political appreciation, this campaign proved to be a failure. Completely defeated at Quebracho Herrado, where many of his officers and supporters were killed, Lavalle escaped from the federal army towards the North, and was killed at Jujuy near the Bolivian border. Thus, the Unitarians had to wait ten more years until they had another opportunity to drive Rosas away. In the meantime, most of them stayed at the neighbouring city of Montevideo, resisting the siege Rosas had imposed to the town which lasted nearly eight years. For this reason Montevideo was called "The New Troy".

But the country was growing tired of Rosas, with no manifest desire for political organization or progress. So, some of his former supporters betrayed him and under the manoeuvre of General Urquiza, governor of the Entre Ríos province, a 50,000 men army was gathered with the support of the Brazilian army and marched against Buenos Aires. Rosas was beaten at the battle of Caseros and forced to move to England, where he survived working as a farmer until his death in 1883. His coffin was brought back from England in 1990 and lies at the Recoleta whitin the family vault.

Even though all were together to push Rosas away and Urquiza deliberately proposed a policy of forgiveness, soon disturbances reappeared. Buenos Aires split from the Confederacy. After four years of fighting, Buenos Aires under the command of General Mitre, defeated Urquiza hus settling their differences, accepted the new Constitution (which with certain amends it is he one still in use nowadays), and gave an energetic step forward for the definitive organization of the nation. Mitre was appointed President and sent his army to end with all the belligerent opposition in the provinces.

n the meantime, Paraguay under the rule of the López family, had become a powerful and organized country with the first railroad in Latin America and a strong and well organized army.

The boundary between Paraguay and Brazil had been a troublesome issue from colonial times and now an international conflict over this subject had arisen. Paraguay asked the Argentine government, for permission to pass its army through our country, permission that General Mitre naturally denied. Francisco Solano López, the strong man in Paraguay invaded Corrientes (north of Argentina), so there was no other possibility but to declare war. Then, Argentina, Brazil and Uruguay formed the Triple Alliance and attacked Paraguay in a long and unpopular war, which finally destroyed the neighbour country after killing General López.

Even though this brutal precedent, the war allowed the National Army to be organized under the "sprit de corps" of a new cultivated generation. Sarmiento, the new president after Mitre, was concerned with education, and every possible effort to build schools all over the country was done. He brought to the country, American teachers whom he knew while he was Ambassador to the United States. Nicolás Avellaneda, the next president, was resisted by Mitre's supporters and had to face an enormous and unbalanced economic situation which he could handle *"saving over the hunger and thirstiness of the people"*.

The country progressed. The railroads joined spare lands and immigrants flooded from abroad, mainly Spain and Italy in such a proportion that at the beginning of the 20th century, nearly 30% of the population had not been born here.

One final step to progress was the move towards the south, the Patagonia, conquering new lands by means of a military expedition driven by General Roca known as "The Conquest of the Desert". With the newly organized army and the help of the Remington rifle, Roca pushed the Indians further south and so he obtained millions of acres, which were distributed among the landowners who had loaned the money for the expedition. This gave immense popularity to Roca who was appointed the next constitutional President. Roca, due to his cunning abilities, was known as "The Fox". He was able to bring the Nation to peace and unparalleled progress, as investors realized the quick development and possibilities of the country. Juárez Celman, his brother-in-law, replaced him, established an oligarchical government and allowed clear advantages to landowners and financial brokers. Political discomfort and improper economic management led to a failed revolution in 1890, where Leandro Alem, Aristóbulo del Valle and Hipólito Yrigoyen (undiscussed leaders of the new popular movement, the Radical Party) compelled people to the streets. Though the rebellion was defeated due to the lack of a proper organization, Juárez Celman was forced to quit, Carlos Pellegrini took office, in one of the most critical economic emergencies in our history. But this elegant and sage lawyer, founder of the exclusive Jockey Club, proved to be a real statesman, "A Captain in the storm" as he was called, and brought the country back to its natural growing condition.

A whole series of conservative presidents, Roca, for the second time, José Evaristo Uriburu, Figueroa Alcorta, Quintana, Luis Sáenz Peña and Victorino de la Plaza, held a continuity in political and economical power, through fraudulent elections, where the Radical Party refused to participate. It was not until 1914 when Roque Sáenz Peña (son of the former president Luis Sáenz Peña, hero of the Pacific war and General of the Peruvian army) established the free, secret and universal vote. This fact, cleared the way to the Radical Party, whose leader Hipólito Yrigoyen, (after the suicide of Leandro Alem) was elected President of the nation. Yrigoyen's first government (1916 – 1922) though popular and democratic was characterized by its neutrality in World War I, its intervention to most provinces and strikes directed by the anarchists that where severely repressed. His follower, Marcelo T. de Alvear, grandson of the hero of the Brazilian war, led a brilliant and progressive government which allowed Yrigoyen to be elected for a second term. But then he was old and lacked the power and wit of previous years, and conducted a series of unpopular measures leading to General José Félix Uriburu's revolution in 1930. So it started a series of putsches that made the Army referee in Argentinian politics. Uriburu only lasted two years and passed the torch to General Justo who inherited a complicated economic worldwide situation (1930).

Pilar Church

Justo and his Vice-President Julio Roca, son of the former president, made a deal with England and gave this country some commercial advantages on behalf of their preferences for our beef and grains. This led to a series of angry discussions that ended with the life of Senator Bordaberry, who was killed inside the very Parliament House during a debate, while defending Senator Lisandro de la Torre.

Ortiz replaced Justo after fraudulent elections. But Ortiz died from his diabetes and his Vice President, Castillo seized power, maintaining Argentina's neutrality during WW II. Then after a series of conservative governments, Colonel Perón, a nationalist officer admirer of Mussolini and former Work Minister, was popularly elected and proposed a new way in politics, mainly demagogic. He was supported by his second wife, the actress Evita Duarte who began assisting individual claims, gaining the favour of the lower classes. She died young at 33, from a gynecological cancer, at the top of her popularity. Perón went on with his government, but his confrontation with the Church, the political and military establishment plus the economical detriment of his last years, led to a revolution conducted by General Lonardi. Lonardi wanted to consolidate democracy without forbidding any political party. But his fellow officers did not share the same idea. So he had to resign and General Aramburu climbed to the Presidency and allowed elections with the abstention of the Peronist Party which gave Dr. Frondizi, a former Radical leader, its vote. Though he was the head of a progressive and liberal government, the Army disapproved of his approach to the Peronist and Communist parties as well as his policy concerning the oil industry. He was politically under strong pressure and had to give way to Dr. Guido, who was dependant on the Army's supervision.

New elections were called with the new abstention of the Peronist Party. Dr. Illia, a physician with a long Radical membership, was elected with only the 25% of the votes. His government though honest and politically tolerant, could not withstand pressures and a new *coup d'eta* conducted General Onganía to the Presidency in 1966.

The rest is present history. Perón returned to the government after 17 years in exile, and died during his third Presidency, leaving his unable wife, Isabel, in his place. Under the influence f José López Rega, a former policeman, who led the right wing of the Peronist Party, the ountry went into a non-declared civil war, with the active participation of the Army, onducted by General Videla, Admiral Massera and Brigadier Agosti. Eight years of dictatorial overnment began with its economical and social consequence of 30,000 missing people.

his is a brief summary of our history. Many of our great men here buried are to be honoured nd remembered.

et them rest in peace.

The Pilar Church and the Recoleta Cemetery

This church of beautiful colonial style was projected by Rev. Klaus and Rev. Wolf and built by Andrés Bianchi, all Jesuits who had previously worked in the Metropolitan Cathedral.
uan Narbona, a rich merchant, said to be a smuggler, gave all the money for its construction. The church was finished by October 1732.

n 1822, Governor Martín Rodríguez and his Minister Rivadavia - ordered the construction of this cemetery called Northern Cemetery over the fields of the Recoleta Fathers, to Mr. Prosper Catelin, a French engineer.

n 1863, the bishop of Buenos Aires retired his blessed condition after President Mitre ordered he burial of a well-known mason, blessing that has not and will not be recovered.
During 1888, the Major of Buenos Aires, Torcuato de Alvear, reconstructed the deteriorated cemetery, with the help of architect Busschiazzo, to its present extension.

n 1946 it was declared National Monument and in 1949 changed its former name to The Recoleta, as known nowadays.

Juan Bautista ALBERDI
Lawyer and musician
1810 - 1884

Curiously, even though this statesman, journalist and lawyer lived half of his life outside the country, he was the one who settled the basis and guidelines of our National Constitution. Born in Tucumán, he had to escape from the Rosas' regime and finished his days in Paris as a diplomat.

He held an extensive and interesting epistolary discussion with President Sarmiento over the political arrangement of the country and wrote a book disapproving the war with Paraguay. He was a gifted musician as well.

Since 1990 his body rests at the Cathedral of his native town.

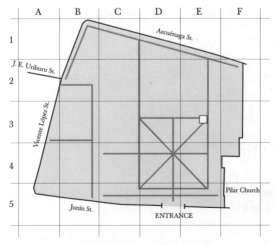

Juan Bautista Alberdi - E3

David ALLENO
A life for a tomb

Alleno used to work at this cemetery. It is said that he saved money all his life to buy a vault here. He travelled to Italy where he commended his statue to Canepa who represented him just in the way he used to work for many years at the Recoleta.

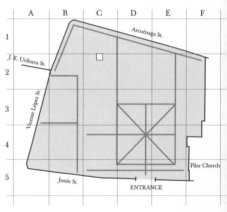

David Alleno - C2

Emma Nicolay de CAPRILE
Teacher of teachers
? - 1884

She was a Hungarian lady married to an Italian who came to Argentina to work as a teacher. She became the promoter of a whole generation of teachers at the Normal School Nº 1. Hipólito Yrigoyen, the future President of the Nation, was present at her funeral.

This beautiful statue, by Della Cárcova, shows Mrs. Caprile teaching his nephew to read.

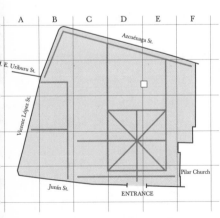

Emma Nicolay de Caprile - E2

Valentín ALSINA
1802 - 1869

Adolfo ALSINA
1829 - 1877

The wrong artist

Valentín Alsina was a young lawyer who despite the fact that he was married to the daughter of one of Rosas' friends, was forced to run away towards Uruguay to save his life. After Caseros' battle (Rosas' defeat), he fulfilled various services for the Buenos Aires province government and for the arising national organization.

He had the honour of taking the oath as Vice-President to his son Adolfo, who died while he was creating a defensive line against the indians attack. This monument was made 40 years after his death. Despite the fact that sculptor Bonet's project was chosen, she could not finish the work due to technical problems and it was concluded by the Argentinian artist Duggon. Mrs Bonet, notwithstanding her dismissal, the day after the sculpture was exhibited for the first time, stamped her signature at its basis, that solely belongs to her, in dreams and ambition.

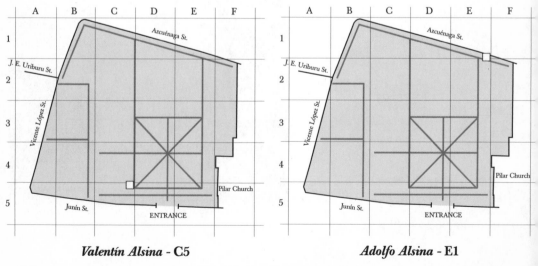

Valentín Alsina - C5

Adolfo Alsina - E1

Marcelo T. de ALVEAR
An opera singer, first lady of the nation
1868 - 1942

After rendering services at the Spanish Army, General José María de Alvear (1789 – 1853) returned to his native country to serve in the Independence wars together with San Martín, to whom he soon left apart. He was responsible for Montevideo's capture and was General-in-Chief during the war against Brazil. His son Torcuato (1822 – 1890) became the first Major of Buenos Aires and was the one who ordered the reconstruction of this cemetery in 1881.

His son, Marcelo Torcuato de Alvear was President of the Nation and relevant authority of the Radical Party. He fell in love with a famous opera singer, Regina Pacini, whom he followed through the world for eight years until she finally accepted his marriage proposal. She was known for her charity activities, as it is remembered in the various bronze plaques in gratitude.

Marcelo's cousin Diego de Alvear, was a powerful landowner. He had this sculpture posing with his daughter made by Roulleau. On one side of the vault, Jorge Luis Borges dedicated a beautiful poem to Elvira de Alvear, his sister.

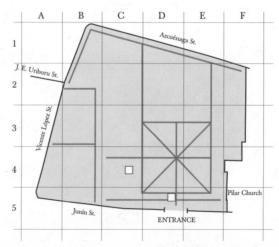

Marcelo T. de Alvear - **D5**
and Diego de Alvear - **C4**

ALZAGA
The wealthiest man of this time.
1756 - 1812

M artín de Alzaga was the wealthiest man of his time (1756 – 1812). However, he did not doubt to offer effort and fortune to fight against the English invaders in 1806 and 1807. As a Spaniard, he remained faithful to the Crown, did not accept the May proposal of our native citizens and conspired or at least was accused of plotting against the new administration. For that reason, he was executed and hanged in Mayo Square. His wife and daughters locked themselves in their house until the end of their lives, and left it only in a last journey at the moment of their deaths to inhabit this mausoleum.

The last one died in 1880, sixty-eight years after Martín de Alzaga's capital punishment.

One of his grandsons, a very wealthy man too, married Felicitas Guerrero, a beautiful young maid, who became the wealthiest woman in Argentina when her husband died towards the end of the 19th century. Enrique Ocampo, in love with the widow, was deceived when he found out that Felicitas was to marry another man and after a fight, he shot her and then found death himself. Both are buried few yards apart, here at the Recoleta.

Her family built a church in her memory, Santa Felicitas, that can be visited in Barracas area.

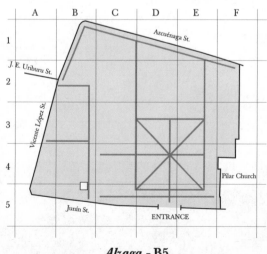

***Alzaga* - B5**

ANCHORENA
As wealthy as they could be

At the beginning of the 20th century, there was a common saying "as rich as an Anchorena". And so they were. The founders of the family, related to Juan Manuel de Rosas, had large extensions of land, which were increased through businesses, pre-arranged marriages and hard-working to nearly 2,000,000 acres at the turning of the 19th century.

Tomás Manuel de Anchorena (1873 – 1847) was one of the signers of our Independence, Governor of Buenos Aires and supporter of Dorrego and his cousin Rosas. Many members of the family held important social and political functions. Some of them were famous for their fashionable and sophisticated way of life.

Fabián Gómez Anchorena gave a blank bank note to Alfonso XIII, King of Spain, for his coronation. He received on his behalf the title of "Conde del Castaño". Fabián Gómez lost all his properties and died in poverty.

Aaron Anchorena was, together with Jorge Newberry, the first man in Latin America to cross the River Plate flying in a balloon.

Joaquín Anchorena was Major of Buenos Aires and President of the elegant Jockey Club, whose building can be seen neighbouring the French and Brazilian Embassy. They held many mausoleums and vaults over the cemetery, some of them as splendorous, as their way of life.

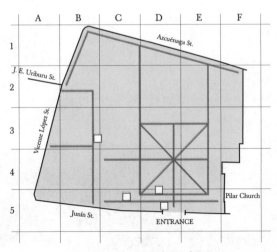

Anchorena - **B3 / C5 / D5**

Pedro Eugenio ARAMBURU
Under tons of concrete
1903 - 1970

Aramburu was one of the generals that defeated General Perón in the 1955 coup d'état. Perón went into exile for 17 years to return and become President for a third time. After his death, he was buried in the Chacarita Cemetery (not here with Evita). Some years ago, his tomb was profaned and his hands were cut and robbed. Mistery stands unsolved to the present.

Aramburu followed Lonardi as President after the Revolution. He gave way to a new democratic government led by Dr. Frondizi, after an election that forbade the Peronist movement.

In 1970, Aramburu was kidnapped and murdered by a terrorist group. His body, was buried in this cemetery, and it was robbed some years later, then it was returned as a piece of exchange, to recover Evita's body (also disappeared during years). To prevent new profanations, architect Bustillo – the same one who designed the Llao Llao Hotel in Bariloche – together with the sculptor Della Cárcova built up this monument upon tons of concrete so that General Aramburu may rest eternally in peace.

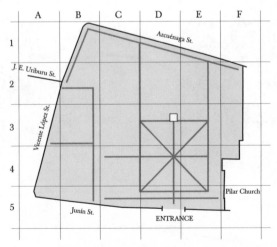

Pedro Eugenio Aramburu - D3

ATUCHA
The grief of a wife

T he Atuchas were wealthy landowners with vast extensions of land in the Province of Buenos Aires, especially in the north where a town was named after them.

orge Atucha (1795 – 1863) was a fervent anti-Rosas man; he helped to escape several intellectuals rom Buenos Aires who were persecuted by the regime. He loved horse racing and even today . Turf Classic is ran under his name.

f you watch this mausoleum made by Mrs. Lima de Atucha just in the centre of the cemetery, n remembrance of her husband you will see at the top, the image of a woman, her face covered y a piece of cloth, hiding her grief.

he door of the Atucha Sarassa tomb was made in France. This vault was designed by Rene ergent, the same architect that built the Errázuriz Palace in Libertador Avenue, today the National Museum of Decorative Arts.

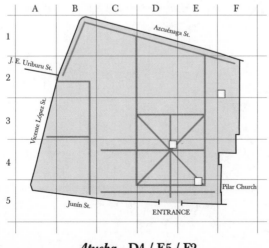

Atucha - **D4 / E5 / F2**

AVELLANEDA
Martyr of Metan
1813 - 1841

Marco Avellaneda (1813 – 1841) was a brilliant young Governor of the province of Tucumán, opponent to Rosas' regime. He was defeated in the battle of Quebracho Herrado, persecuted, beheaded in Metan and his head exposed at the town central square. Once his remains were recovered, he was buried in this monument ordered to sculptor Biggi by his son Nicolás (1837 – 1885), who turned to be President of the Nation in 1874.

His other son – named Marco as well – (1839 – 1903), represented his native province as Senator for more than 15 years. He requested the construction of his tomb to the sculptor Cardona, who represented a weeping woman mourning his death.

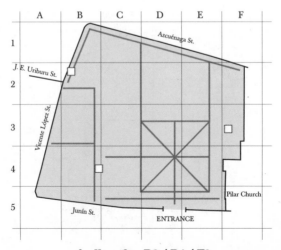

Avellaneda - **B2 / B4 / F3**

José Toribio AYERZA
Victims of the Mafia
1815 - 1884

Ayerza was a physician of Basque origin, the first professional to practise a tracheotomy, procedure that during diphtheria epidemic saved many lives.

In front of this splendid sculpture, Sansebastino' s work, it is the family vault where in 1935 a huge crowd gathered to pay the last respects to one of Ayerza' s grandsons, killed after being kidnapped by the Sicilian mafia in our country.

The family continues nowadays as physicians, lawyers, landowners and financial entrepreneurs.

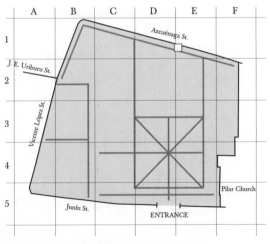

José Toribio Ayerza - E1

Pierre BENOIT
The never crowned Louis XVII
? - 1853

He called himself the Dolphin of France, the never crowned Luis XVII, presumably dead at the Du Temple Prison, but mysteriously appeared in these lands where he devoted to architecture and painting. The original design of this cemetery and the Buenos Aires Cathedral's frontispiece are among his works. They were done together with engineer Catelin. He worked undisturbed, during 20 years as Chief of Topography of Rosas' administration. Benoit died as mysteriously as he had lived, maybe poisoned with arsenic by an enigmatic French who soon after his death vanished into thin air.

Curiously, the last picture he had painted was one of Marie Antoinette with whom he had a remarkable resemblance.

His son, named after him, was an architect too, author of more than 500 works, among them La Plata Cathedral and Luján Basilic.

The Caliper and Compass show his undoubtedly masonic condition. The sculpture is made by Rafael Hernández.

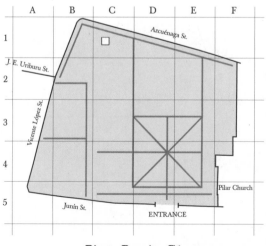

Pierre Benoit - C1

Federico BRANDSEN
When Napoleon gave you an order you did not argue...
1785 - 1827

He was a brave French soldier who fought under Napoleon. He was invited by Rivadavia to our country. Upon his arrival he joined San Martín's army during the Chilean and Peruvian independence campaigns. Back in Argentina, he participated in the Brazilian war. During the decisive battle of Ituzaingo, his superior – General Alvear – who by the crooked purposes of fate was buried just in front of Brandsen, – ordered him a suicidal charge. Brandsen objected the order, to what Alvear answered: "When Napoleon gave you an order, you did not argue".

Brandsen exclaimed: "I know I am going to die, but I shall fulfill my duties as imparted". And, alas!, he did, dying as he had foretold, at the front of his charging regiment.

The sculpture, ordered by Alvear's son, was done by Carlos Romairone and has been declared National Monument.

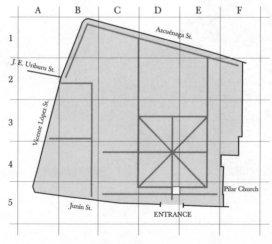

Federico Brandsen - D5

LA MUNICIPALIDAD DE BUENOS AIRES
RECONOCIDA A LOS SERVICIOS DEL
CORONEL FEDERICO DE BRANDSEN

BRITISH TOMBS
"Sacred to the memory"

In 1840 there were 15,000 foreign people in Buenos Aires. 3500 were British; they comprised the biggest and strongest economical group of the city.

Many of them were protestants and were buried in the community cemetery which was originally behind the Socorro church.

Between 1821 and 1833, 668 bodies were buried. The most important bodies were De Cesar Augusto Rodwey – Plenipotentiary Minister of USA –, James Beavans – Carlos Pellegrini's grandfather –, James Faunch (owner of a luxurious hotel in BA) and William Parish Robertson's wife (powerful businessman who left interesting writings about River Plate's traditions) besides the already mentioned Elisa Brown and her fiancé Francis Drumond. All these tombs had disappeared today but it is in the Recoleta where there still remain graves of the Catholic British Community, especially Irish, who came to our lands running away from hunger and the oppression of their natal land, to settle down and grow up between us, persisting their last names until these days.

Many of their tombs are crowned with a Celtic cross, others have angels and cypresses, typical cemetery tree. All of them start with a "Sacred to the memory..."

Gerald Dillon was a merchant. He installed the first beer factory in Buenos Aires. His brother fought together with Lavalle.

Edward Casey was a strong financier and farm producer, who founded prosperous colonies in Buenos Aires.

The **Mullhalls** were editors of the "Standard", the English community newspaper during the first half of 19th century. They introduced cotton to the country.

Murray was a notable pharmaceutic.

The **Murtaghs** became doctors. One of their descendents was the promoter of neonatology in the country.

The **Duggans** were landowners. Many of the first Scottish and Irish dedicated to sheep breeding in Buenos Aires.

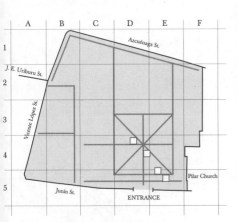

British Tombs - **D4 / E5**

A LA LUZ DEL 9 FEBRERO DEL 11 DE JUNIO DEL 26
DE JULIO DEL AÑO 1826 EN LAS AGUAS DEL PLATA
Y DEL 9 DE FEBRERO DE 1827 EN LAS AGUAS DEL URUGUAY
CONTEMPLO VICTORIOSAS
A LAS NAVES QUE LA REPUBLICA ARGENTINA
CONFIARA AL ALMIRANTE BROWN EN AUXILIO DE
LA INDEPENDENCIA DE UN PUEBLO HERMANO

Admiral William BROWN
Our National Navy heroe
1777 - 1957

Admiral Brown was born in Ireland, even though the plaque wrongly states he was English. Navy hero and founder of our National Navy; a touching fact is that the coffin that keeps his body was made with the bronze of his cannons. Behind him there is a wooden box with the remains of his daughter, Elizabeth, who is said to have committed suicide after the death of her fiancé Captain Drummond, fallen while fighting under her father's command.

This monument and the plaque at its foot were made by the Argentine sculptor Cafferata.

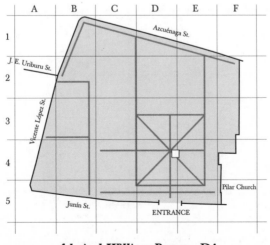

Admiral William Brown - D4

Rufina CAMBACERES
The mysterious lady in white
1884 - 1903

Rufina belonged to a very important family. Her uncle was a well-known politician and her father, Eugenio (1843 – 1888) an outstanding writer who unveiled the social hypocrisy at the end of 19th century. He was married to an actress of Austrian origin, but this marriage was never well seen by the local aristocracy.

On the night Rufina was to celebrate her 19th birthday, she was found dead without any apparent cause. Buried promptly, the cemetery wardens noticed after some days, in shock, that the coffin had moved. The moment it was open they saw the scratches and hits on Rufina's face in a desperate attempt to escape.

She had been buried alive, presumably of catalepsy.

Nobody knows for sure what really happened, even though she had been examined by three physicians.

Her family chose Rich Aigner to create this Art Deco sculpture, crowded with plenty of floral arrangements, as a pretending guidance for Rufina's opening Heaven's doors, leaving behind her awesome last moments.

Perhaps, Rufina is the mysterious lady in white which many people swear to have seen wandering at night near the cemetery.

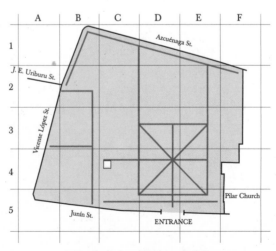

Rufina Cambaceres - C4

Gen. Luis María CAMPOS
Family of soldiers
1838 - 1907

General of the Nation during Paraguayan War and the Desert Campaign. His monument was made by Jules Felix Coutan in Paris. Some metres away, his brother Manuel has another sculpture by Llaneses. Two other brothers Julio and Gaspar were colonels.

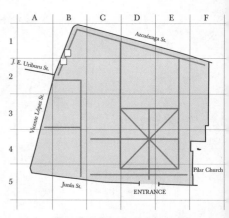

Gen. Luis María Campos - B2
and Gen. Manuel Campos - B1

Bonifacio DEL CARRIL
"Not a happy marriage"
1798 - 1883

He was the first Constitutional Vice-President of the Nation under General Urquiza government. This monument ordered by his wife to sculptor Romairone, continues the marriage lifelong misunderstandings as his wife preferred not to stare, for the rest of eternity, in the same direction as his husband does.

It is said that Del Carril refused to pay his wife's debts through a letter published in every newspaper. Mrs. Del Carril never spoke again to her husband during her life.

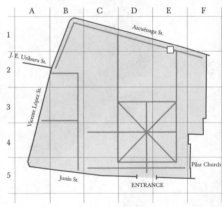

Bonifacio del Carril - E1

CROCIATTI

Perche, Perche...

1945 - 1970

This young and beautiful maid was killed in an avalanche during her honeymoon. Being the only offspring, her parents honoured her beloved daughter building this vault in the particular style she cultivated. The statue was commended to Villarich who depicted her from ancient photos in the company of her predilect dog, Sabu, who had died ten years before. His father, a famous stylist, wrote a poem in Italian, distilling his sorrow.

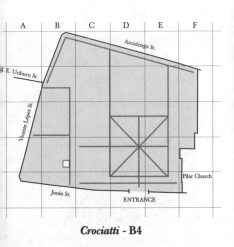

***Crociatti* - B4**

PANTHEON OF OUTSTANDING CITIZENS
Pay homage to them

Just like all his brothers and father, Marcos Balcarce (1777 – 1832) started his military career fighting against the Indians. During the English invasions, he was taken prisoner and removed to England, where he was held for some time. Later, he joined the Spanish army against Napoleon and finally returned to Argentina where he accompanied San Martín during the Chilean campaign. He was minister of Rivadavia, Vicente López y Planes and Rosas.

Just at the moment of his death, Juan Manuel de Rosas decided to keep this parcel, near the centre of the cemetery, to bury outstanding citizens.

Neighbouring General Balcarce's, you will find the tomb of the first leader of the Patriotic Groups during May 1810, **Cornelio Saavedra** (1761 – 1829), who returned to the country after many years of exile in Chile and lived a humble existence rejecting all kind of honours at the time of his death.

Perdriel became Buenos Aires first Police Chief.

Antonio Sáenz (1780 – 1825) was a priest, and the first Director of Buenos Aires University and one of the writer of the Independence Declaration.

Gregorio Funes (1749 – 1829) was Dean of the Córdoba Cathedral (where his remains presently rest) and one of the most enthusiastic promoters of the May Revolution movement.

Peña was a famous educator. Above his tomb, we can see an extraordinary plaque by the Italian artist Livi depicting the Biblical scene "let children come to me".

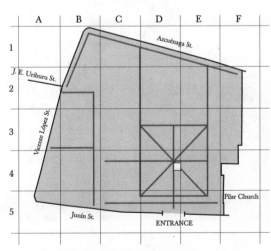

Pantheon of Outstanding Citizens - D4

DEVOTO
The lost palace

A wealthy Italian family, devoted to commerce and industry. Devoto built a magnificent palace to accommodate the Italian king during his visit to Buenos Aires, even though the king never came, and Devoto never inhabited his palace. The building was demolished in 1930.

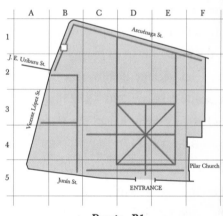

Devoto - **B1**

Remedios de ESCALADA
San Martín's wife
1797 - 1825

She married the 34-year-old Lieutenant Colonel José de San Martin when she was only 15. Remedios belonged to a wealthy family. Her brothers served with honour under San Martin's command. She died in 1825 from tuberculosis, and she saw her husband for the last time nearly 6 years before.

San Martín arrived shortly after her death to order this tomb, where he declared his affection for "his wife and friend" and parted to France with their only daughter Mercedes, never to see this place again. San Martín's parents were buried few yards away. Now they remain at San Martín's birthplace in Misiones.

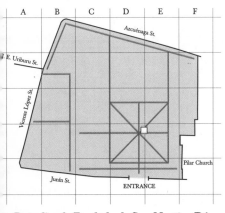

Remedios de Escalada de San Martín - **D4**

Luis DORREGO
The night chevaliers
1784 - 1852

Brother of Manuel Dorrego and partner of Juan Manuel de Rosas, Luis Dorrego was extremely wealthy. He left his fortune to his daughters, when his wife died, her corpse was kidnapped by the self called "Night Chevaliers", who claimed an extraordinary ransom.

Discovered by the police, (the coffin never left the cemetery) the crime went unpunished as the Penal Code at that time did not establish corpse kidnapping as a mischief.

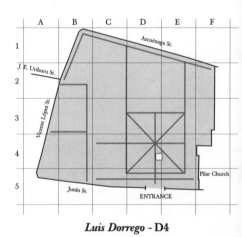

Luis Dorrego - **D4**

Cnel. Manuel DORREGO
Two carnation (one red, one white...)
1828

Independence hero, known for his courage, beloved by his soldiers but detested by his superior due to his sober character, he became, after being vanished to Baltimore (USA) the leader of the Federal Party. He was defeated by General Lavalle and was immediately executed. His body was recovered and was solemnly buried one year later, by his friend Juan Manuel de Rosas.

Over his coffin two carnations, one red, one white, always lie as symbol of goodwill between brothers.

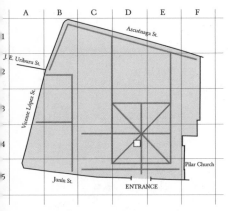

*Cnel. Manuel Dorrego- **D4***

Eva DUARTE de PERON
There are always flowers at her door
1919 - 1952

This 33-year-old artist died while her husband was President of the Nation. In her short life, she earned admiration and visceral hate as well. Once dead and embalmed, her corpse turned into a symbol and millions mourned her absence. After her husband left the country, her body was strictly guarded, even though flowers always appeared at the door where she was secretly hidden. So after a misfortunate event - one of her guards wrongly shot his own wife while hiding her body in their house. The military government decided to get rid of her coffin and sent it secretly to an Italian cemetery in Milan, where she was left in peace for nearly 20 years, until a new military regime gave it back to General Perón during his Spanish exile.

Once it was brought back to the country, the coffin was kidnapped another time and recovered again. It was given to her sisters who introduced it to their vault, where she could finally find eternal peace under tons of concrete. There are always flowers at these doors. Always.

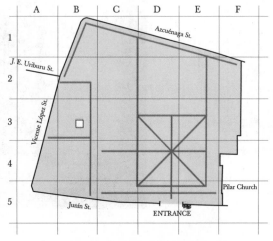

Eva Duarte de Perón - **B3**

Ramón FALCON and Juan LARTIGAU
1855 - 1909   1889 - 1909
Dead by an anarchist bomb

R amón Falcón was chief of the Police Department, known for his aggressive attitude towards anarchist riots, so common at the beginning of the century. He was killed by a bomb thrown by a young Russian acrat that immediately ended his life as well as that of his twenty-year-old secretary, Juan Lartigau. A National collect allowed these monuments by Drivier and Pynot to keep their memory alive.

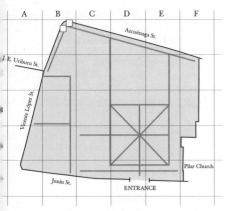

Ramón Falcón and Juan Lartigau - B1

Father FAHY
Beloved by the Irish community
1805 - 1871

F ahy was an Irish priest, famous among his fellow citizens who commended this statue to his honour made in Ireland by Earley.

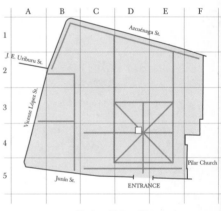

Father Fahy - **D4**

FIRPO
The savage bull from the Pampas
1894 - 1960

The savage Pampa's bull". Famous boxer who lost the world title fighting against Jack Dempsey in 1929, and drove Dempsey out of the ring with one of his demolishing blows. His wife ordered this monument to Perlotti, and depicted him in his gown as if confronting death in his last round.

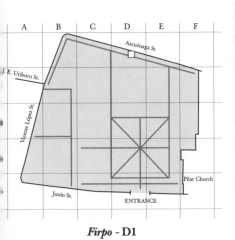

Firpo - **D1**

Luz María GARCIA VELLOSO
The maiden and the poems
1910 - 1925

G arcia Velloso was a famous play writer whose daughter died from leukemia whe only fifteen. Several friends wrote touching poems in her remembrance.

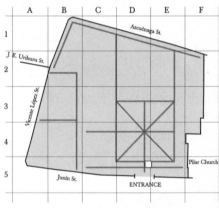

García Velloso - D5

Alfred GATH
(Gonzalez Kondrich vault)
Returning from the valley of the death
1852 - 1936

O wner of the world famous Gath and Chaves mall. He is said to be buried in a coffin with an electric opener in his hands in case he wakes from death. Something we presume he has not used to the present time.

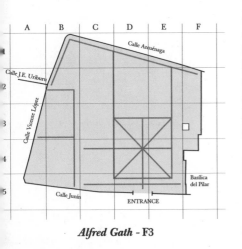

Alfred Gath - **F3**

Gen. Tomás GUIDO
San Martín's best friend
1788 - 1866

Gen. Guido was San Martin's best friend; he followed him to Chile and Peru and afterwards served in Simón Bolivar's army. He came back to the country and served as a diplomat under Rosas' regime.

His son, the poet Guido Spano built this cavern with his own hands.

Gen. Guido's remains were transferred to the Cathedral, next to his senior officer and friend.

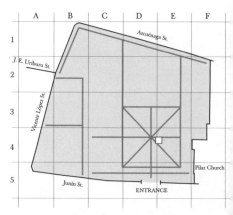

Gen. Tomás Guido - E4

Juan Galo LAVALLE
If he wakes up, tell him his country loves him
1797 - 1841

He was a gallant general who served with uncommon courage during the Independence and Brazilian wars. He headed the revolt against Dorrego and ordered his execution thus beginning twenty years of civil wars. In 1839 he stood against Rosas, and he was defeated and killed in his way to exile. A group of loyal followers guarded his remains until he was buried in Potosí, Bolivia. During 1863 his bones returned to his native land, where a grenadier (his regiment), who resembles the General (Perlotti's work), keeps eternal guard.

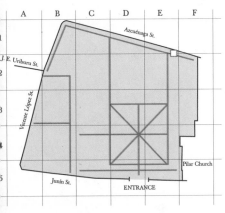

Juan Galo Lavalle - E1

LONARDI
"Not winners, not losers"
1896 - 1956

G eneral Lonardi headed the revolt that drove away President Juan Domingo Perón during 1955. His desire was to reconcile the Nation. But his fellow officers wished to vanish the Peronist Party, so he had to resign as President. He died soon after. At this place (Rovati's work), General Paz and his wife used to be buried, and they were returned to their native town, Córdoba. Now General Lonardi rests here in peace.

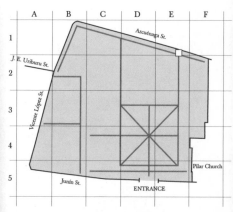

Lonardi - E1

Ramón LOPEZ LECUBE
Lola Mora's statue
1852 - 1912

L ópez Lecube was a wealthy landowner and lawyer who asked the known Argentinian sculptor, Lola Mora, the statue for his vault. Lola Mora is the author of the fountain known as "The Nereidas" – popularly known under her name, placer at the Southern Riverside. This is one of the very few works which she signed with her husband's name.

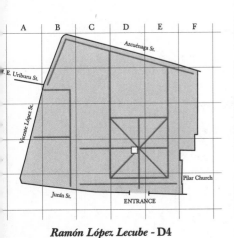

Ramón López Lecube - **D4**

MASONIC TOMBS
This cemetery is not a blessed land

Recoleta cemetery is not a blessed land. When monsignor Aneiros was forced by President Mitre to accept the burial inside Recoleta of a famous mason, he deprived it from his blessing. That is the reason why there is abundance of tombs with masonic symbols. Needless to say, several presidents and ministers, especially during the 19th century and beginning of 20th, do not bear crosses in their tombs (like Mitre, Sarmiento, Avellaneda, Yrigoyen, Del Carril).

The lodge "Obediencia a la Ley" (Obedience to the Law) was founded in approximately 1880. President Sarmiento belonged to it as well as José Hernández – author of the "Martín Fierro" – and Hipólito Yrigoyen. We see the habitual symbols associated with death (owl, clepsydra, inverted torchs) and inside it, other masonic symbols, as the triangle, the sun and the eye.

Some other tombs are pyramids as the one of Mendoza Paz – founder of the Animal Protection Society – where a statement reads: "There is nothing here, just powder and bones".

The Egyptian style seen in some other tombs may be imputed to a masonic origin or to a fashion that existed around the 1920's, when Tutankamon's tomb was discovered.

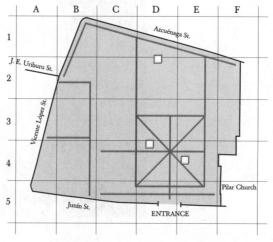

Masonic Tombs - D2 / D4 / E4

MASSONE
A promised land
1863 - 1920

I talian philanthropist and mason as well, newspaperman and founder of a chemical laboratory. This is a brilliant monument by Biggi.

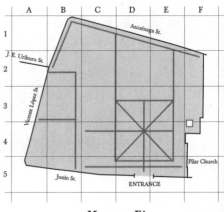

Massone - **F4**

MAUSOLEUM

ausoleos was a Greek king, after his death, his mourning wife Artemisa built one of the seven wonders of the ancient world to his honour and then burnt his body into ashes and drank them with wine.
At this cemetery, you can appreciate various of these momuments made by wives in homage to their beloved husbands.

- Graciarena
- González Borrega
- Godin's work
- Perlotti's work

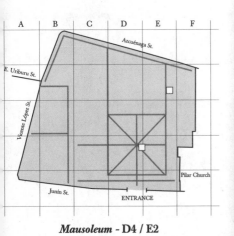

*Mausoleum - **D4 / E2***

Graciarena's Mausoleum.

MITRE
"Let me die as a Roman"
1821 - 1906

He said these words when hit in his head by a bullet during the siege of Buenos Aires. But he did not die then, though he always had to wear a hat to cover this scar for the rest of his long life.

Poet, writer and historian, Mitre translated into Spanish, Dante's Divine Comedy. He learned Italian while fighting with Garibaldi at the siege of Montevideo.

General-in-chief during the Paraguayan war and President of the Nation, as a journalist he directed "La Nación", senior newspaper of the country.

Though through his law the cemetery lost its blessed condition, Mitre, a confessed mason, died in the faith of his seniors.

This beautiful tomb is the work of Edgardo Rubino.

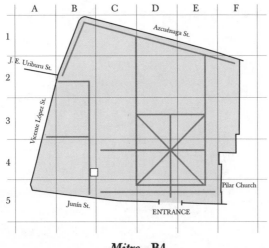

Mitre - B4

Carlos MORRA
The Prince of the architects
1854 - 1926

Prince Morra was educated in Italy and after his service in the Italian army as a specialist in fortresses, he came to Argentina and became the first President of the Architect Central Society. He built this tomb with the family herald, when his daughter, Baby Morra, as he called her, died in Paris at the age of twenty.

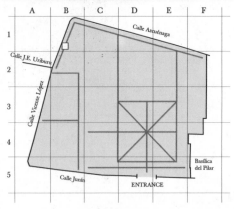

Carlos Morra- **B1**

OLIVERA CISNETTO
A priceless statue
1843 - 1918

Olivera belonged to a wealthy family, founder of the "Sociedad Rural" and owner of vast extensions of lands. He commended this vault to Enrico Fontona whose son Lucio, the famous sculptor, participated in this final and marvellous design.

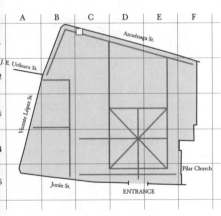

Olivera Cisnetto - **C1**

ORTIZ BASUALDO
The biggest vault in the cemetery

Wealthy descendants from Luis Dorrego, who owned the palace which is now the French embassy. They made this monumental statue copying the Montanari vault in Staglieno cemetery (Genoa, Italy), representing the biblical passage of the virtuous virgins.

The memorah might represent their Jewish ancestry.

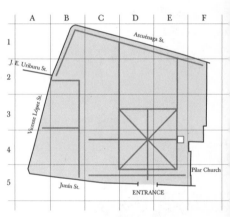

Ortiz Basualdo - E4

Juan José PASO
1758 - 1833

H e was one of the members of the 1810 May Council, our first step in the march towards the separation from Spain, as well as writer of the Independence Declaration in 1816.

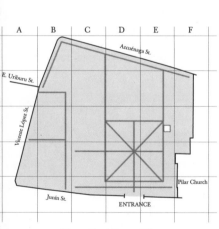

Juan José Paso - E3

PANTHEON OF PARAGUAYAN WARRIOR.
Old soldiers never die, they just disappear

The courage and the dignity of these warriors, most of them young Buenos Aire officers, allowed to keep the discipline of the troop, which was gained by the respec and admiration of their subordinates.

These officers led their soldiers to hard won victories during the Paraguayan campaign, man died in battle, others after years of honorable service.

Díaz, Mayorga, Oris de Roa, Damianovich and the one-handed notable painter Cándido Lópe are, among the dozens, buried here.

Victory stands above them and two bronze soldiers keep eternal guard to these heroes.

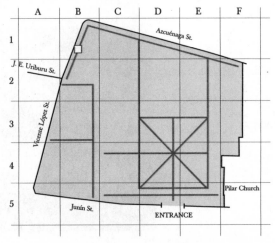

Pantheon of Paraguayan Warriors - B1

José C. PAZ
The most beautiful monument
1842 - 1912

P erhaps this is the most beautiful monument in the cemetery: two huge angels guard the entrance while a third one shows the way to Heaven. This art piece belongs to Frenchman Jules Felix Coutan, and it was ordered by José C. Paz after his son's death.

José C. Paz was the founder of the newspaper "La Prensa".

The building, where the newspaper is published even today, is a beautiful piece of architecture as well as his former private residence in front of San Martín Square, near Florida Street, at the present time belonging to the Military Circle.

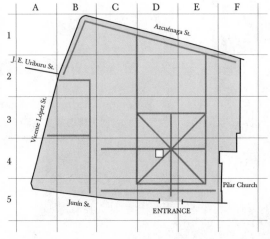

José Camilo Paz - D4

Carlos PELLEGRINI
"A captain in the storm"
1846 - 1906

Great politician and economist, he was President of the Republic in one of the mos dramatic moments of our country.

Juárez Celman had resigned in 1890 after a popular riot and the country had to face urgen economic commitments. Pellegrini managed to solve these problems and led to a new development period.

He founded the exclusive Jockey Club and he was its first President. In front of the Jockey Club headquarter, there stands a magnificent statue of Pellegrini, done by Jules Felix Coutan just near the French and the Brazilian Embassies. This monument was commended to Mercive by his followers.

Paul Groussac issued the term "captain in the storm" to summarize his political abilities.

His father, a French engineer, was also a gifted painter.

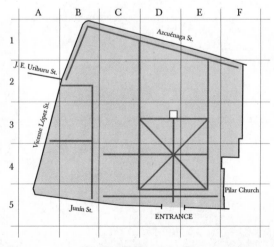

***Carlos Pellegrini* - D3**

Patricio PERALTA RAMOS
1814 - 1887

The Peralta Ramos was a wealthy family of landowners, founders of Mar del Plata seaside resort. One of his grandsons, Patricio Peralta Ramos, was the first editor of the newspaper "La Razón". The huge truncated column that crowns this old building represents death that leaves our earthly works unfinished.

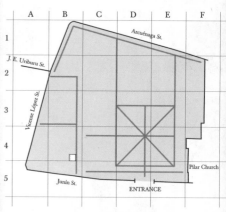

Patricio Peralta Ramos - B4

RAMOS MEJIA

Ancient and venerable family

One of the most ancient and venerable families in Argentina. Landowners, soldiers against the Rosas' regime, famous doctors and writers as well, were some of the members of this extraordinary family that continues up to our days.

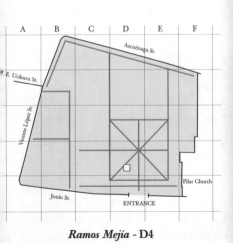

Ramos Mejía - **D4**

Juan Martín de PUEYRREDON
Supreme Director
1777 - 1850

Prilidiano PUEYRREDON
Outstanding Painter
1813 - 1870

H e was a distinguished military man during the English invasions and our Independence war. While being Director, the Independence Declaration was signed. He gave an unconditional support to San Martín's campaigns, and he was his friend too.

His son Prilidiano (1813 – 1870) was a famous architect, designer of the "Quinta de Olivos" (President of the Nation's official private residence), the May Pyramid, and by far, the most outstanding Argentinian painter of 19th century. The house which belonged to the family is still kept in San Isidro, as a museum.

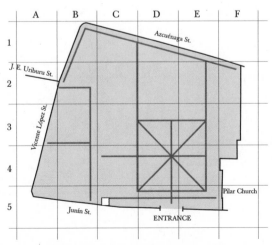

Juan Martín de Pueyrredón - C5

Juan PUJOL
First mail stamp in the country
1817 - 1861

G overnor of Corrientes province and one of the officers during the Caseros' campaign that ended with Rosas' regime. A plaque remembers him as the promoter of the first mail stamp in Argentina, just 16 years after Rowland Hill.

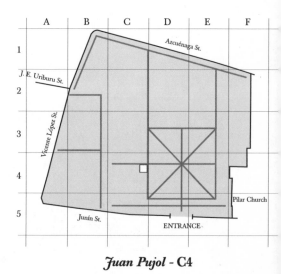

Juan Pujol - C4

Dr. William COLLISBERY RAWSON
Politician and physician
1821 - 1890

E minent doctor and politician of American origin, he was especially interested in public health. He died in Paris, during an eye surgery.

The sculpture was made by Carriere Belleuse, the same that made San Martin's vault at the Cathedral.

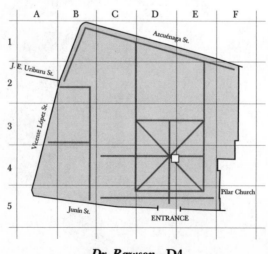

Dr. Rawson - D4

Manuel QUINTANA
The elegant President
1835 - 1906

P resident of Argentina, he died during his administration. The monument that show him elegantly lying, was made by the French artist, Fagelle.

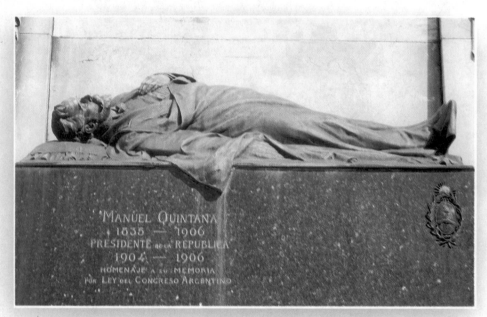

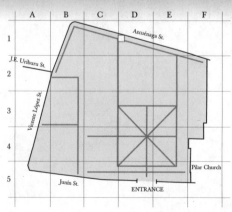

Manuel Quintana - D1

ROVERANO

Embrace a new land

A s thousand of Italians, the Roveranos arrived in Argentina, looking after fortune and peace. They were owners of a well-known café, now gone.

As many immigrants, they wished to embrace a new land of their own.
Now they lost one arm...

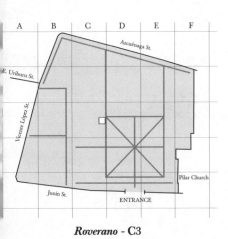

Roverano - **C3**

Gen. Martín RODRIGUEZ
Founder of the Recoleta Cemetery
1771 - 1845

He was Governor of Buenos Aires and founder of the city of Tandil. He was also promoter for the creation of this cemetery. The beautiful sculpture by Arturo Dresco is one of the most elegant art works at the cemetery.

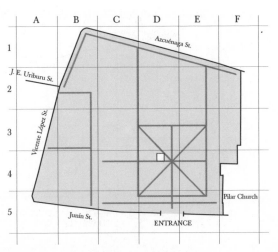

Gen. Martín Rodríguez - D4

Juan Facundo QUIROGA
Standing in front of the Lord
1793 - 1835

L eader of La Rioja province, man of extraordinary courage and great power, was killed during a journey towards the North where he was travelling to settle a provincial quarrel.

He was brought to Buenos Aires and buried in this vault that it is crowned by the image of Sorrowing Mother (Madre Dolorosa), sculptor Tartadini's artwork, representing Facundo's wife, mourning for her husband's death. It was the first sculpture at the Recoleta. This image can be found crowning many others mausoleums along the entire cemetery. Facundo's fame endures up to the present times, mainly because of Sarmiento's book.

The legend says that Facundo is buried standing, following his precise request. That was the way he believed a "macho" man had to face his Creator.

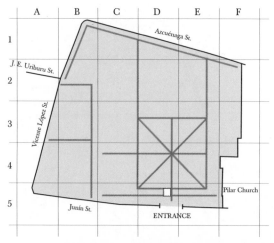

Juan Facundo Quiroga - D5

1890 REVOLUTION
The Radical Party

During Juárez Celman's government, corruption and deceit had reached an intolerabl< level of the opposition gathered around Leandro Alem and Aristóbulo Del Valle, wh< founded the Radical Party.

They confronted Celman's government in a popular revolt that was severally crushed, witl< hundreds of dead people.

Though defeated in the field, they showed Celman's lack of popular support and forced hin< to resign on behalf of his Vice-President Carlos Pellegrini.

Del Valle died soon afterwards and Alem committed suicide. They were succeeded by Alem'< nephew, Hipólito Yrigoyen, who in time became President of the Nation, after the first free< elections. He was twice President, but his second period ended in a coup d'etat that gave way< to the first military President in Argentina (José F. Uriburu). This mausoleum was erected t< bury the radical followers dead during the 1890 Revolution.

Alem, Yrigoyen, Illia and other leaders chose to be buried at the place, Emilio Cantillion'< artwork, turned it into a symbol for their Party.

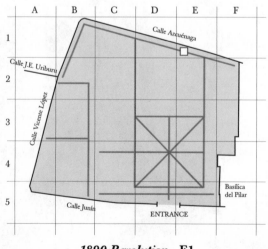

1890 Revolution - E1

Gen. Pablo RICCHIERI
Military Service
1859 - 1936

General of our Nation, he created the Military Service and organized the modern Argentinian Army. In this mausoleum, (Perlotti's artwork), Bernardo de Monteagudo (San Martín's secretary) and Juan O'Brien, (an Irishman who fought during the Chilean and Peruvian campaigns) as well as other heroes of the Nation, are buried here.

At this place Bernardino Rivadavia, first President of the Nation, was previously buried, until he was moved where he now rests in Plaza Once (once called Miserere).

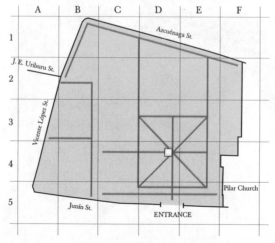

Gen. Pablo Ricchieri - D4

Julio Argentino ROCA
The fox
1843 - 1914

G eneral of the Nation. Twice President of the country. He was one of the most important men who pushed the National progress, by defeating indians and occupying all the Patagonia.

He was called "The fox" due to his cunning political abilities.

Roca is buried with his father, Independence Colonel Segundo Roca – dead during the Paraguayan campaign and with his son, named also after him, who became Vicepresident in 1932.

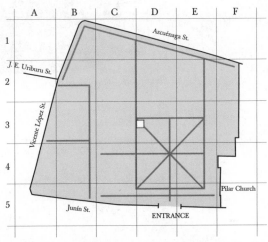

Julio Argentino Roca - **D3**

Juan Manuel de ROSAS
The turning point in history
1793 - 1877

Argentine's history is divided in two major periods: before and after Rosas. The turning point in history is: who supported him and who did not. He ruled the country during twenty years with tough hands, keeping order by repressing sometimes with unnecessary brutality any sign of opposition. But, likewise, he was successful in defending with energy all attempts of foreign countries pressure. General San Martín, in admiration, stated in his will that his bent saber was to be given to Rosas after his death.

Once he was defeated at Caseros, he exiled to England where he made a living working as a farmer as he used to do during his youth.

A namesake grandson became an active progressive governor of Buenos Aires province in 1910. In 1990, Rosas remains were brought to his family vault, where his mother, wife, brothers and grandsons are buried. It is said that when his wife's coffin was opened she was found untouched as if she were sleeping.

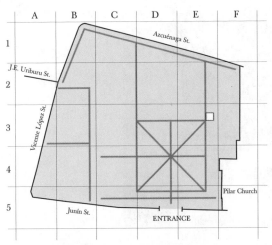

Juan Manuel de Rosas - **E3**

Carlos SAAVEDRA LAMAS
Our First Nobel Prize
1878 - 1959

S aavedra Lamas was our first Peace Nobel Prize in 1936. Due to his work as mediator in the war between Bolivia and Paraguay. He was a descendant of Cornelio Saavedra and was married to a past President's daughter – Roque Sáenz Peña's. Together with him lies a former Buenos Aires Major and leading historian – Carlos Pueyrredón.

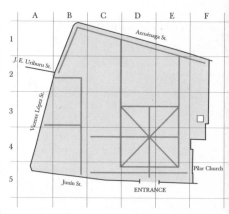

Carlos Saavedra Lamas - F3

Miguel Estanislao SOLER
National Monument
1793 - 1849

San Martín's confident man, he fought by his side in Chile and then became Alvear's Army Major Chief during the Brazilian campaign.

This sculpture is considered a National Monument, Dasso's art piece.

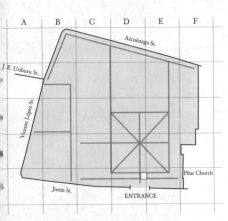

Miguel Estanislao Soler - D5

Luis SAENZ PEÑA   Roque SAENZ PEÑA
1835 - 1587   1851 - 1914
Father and son, Presidents of the Nation

E arnest lawyer, member of the Supreme Court, became President due to the political game of the "Fox" Roca, who, in this way, avoided the presentation of his son Roque Sáenz Peña, who had more progressive ideas. Anyway, the lack of political support, obliged him to resign in 1895 on behalf of his Vicepresident José Evaristo Uriburu.

His son Roque, was the President who gave democracy its full meaning, by allowing the vote to be secret, compulsory and universal. He died during his administration.

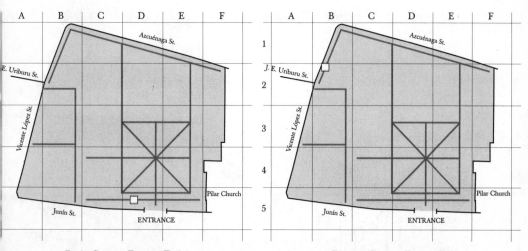

Luis Saenz Peña - D5   *Roque Saenz Peña - B2*

Casto SAENZ VALIENTE
A faithful servant
1796 - 1870

Highly reputed businessman, owner of a huge fortune, and despite he was a very good friend of one of Rosas' brothers – who even left his lands in heritage, had to fly for his life to Uruguay.

Just aside this ancient vault rests an old slave woman Catalina Dugan, who took care of three generations of the Sáenz Valientes. An epitaph praises her loyalness to the family throughout her life.

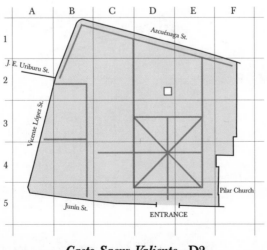

Casto Saenz Valiente - D2

Mariquita SANCHEZ de THOMPSON
Napoleón's granddaughter is said to lie here
1786 - 1868

María de Todos Los Santos Sánchez de Velásquez y Trillo was an outstanding lady that exalted woman's condition in the society of those times. She married her cousin Thompson, and the entire town was shocked because of her courageously standing against her parents refusal. After Thompson's death, she married Mendeville, in charge of the French affairs in Buenos Aires. Despite the fact of her friendship with Rosas, she departed in exile to Montevideo.

During an act offered in her residence, our National Anthem was first heard.

It is said that at this vault, a Napoleon's granddaughter is buried. Isabella Waleski, daughter of Count Waleska, son of Napoleon and the Polish Countess Waleska, died as a child in Buenos Aires while his father led diplomatic charges.

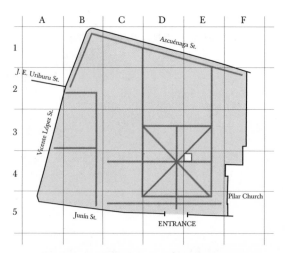

Mariquita Sánchez de Thompson - E4

MARIA
Sanchez de Mendeville
CARITATEM DILEXIT
1784—1868
REQUIESCAT IN PACE

Domingo Fidel SARMIENTO
Dominguito
1847 - 1867

H e was the adopted son of President Domingo Faustino Sarmiento who died during the battle of Curupaití during the Paraguayan war. His father designed this monument to his memory.

Just to its side there are two beautiful angels that belonged to the Ledesma family.

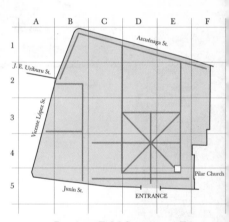

Domingo Fidel Sarmiento - E5

Domingo Faustino SARMIENTO
Ideas are not to be slaughtered
1811 - 1888

Writer, Congressman and President of Argentina. His main target was education. For that purpose he hired foreign teachers, mostly Americans. Sarmiento died in Paraguay. His remains were brought on a ship, and received touching honours all along their way. He himself designed this tomb according to his masonic ideals. It is a milestone for hundreds of students that permanently visit this place to pay homage to this man who fought for freedom of thought above all.

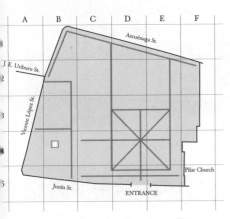

Domingo Faustino Sarmiento - B4

Gen. Isidro SUAREZ
Where Jorge Luis Borges should have been buried
1799 - 1846

I f Borges had not died in Geneve he would lie here together with his mother and grandparents. Isidro Suárez, Independence hero, victorious in the battle of Ayacucho, is buried in the same coffin with his friend Olazábal in eternal friendship beyond death. Colonel Borges died fighting for General Mitre in the 1874 revolt. Both figures deserved poems from their grandson.

Lafinur was a well-known lawyer and writer.

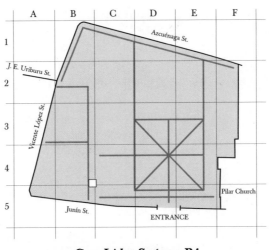

Gen. Isidro Suárez - B4

SPINETTO
Heaven's Door
1835 - 1587

The Spinetto family, like thousands of Italians, arrived in our country with dreams of fortune. Their dreams came true.

First, in the building just where our Congress House stands at the present time. Later, they started a huge market place, in the same ground where the Spinetto Shopping Mall is nowadays, keeping the family name in their honour. This door was made in Italy, depicting Saint George defeating the dragon.

On the wall there are two beautiful plaques remembering the founders and presidents of the family company.

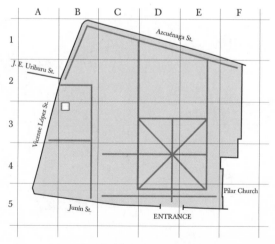

The Spinetto's Door - B3

Virgilio TEDIN
The judge
1850 - 1892

J udge of the Nation, his equity and decency was so outstanding that a popular collection was made in order to built this beautiful monument by San Sebastino.

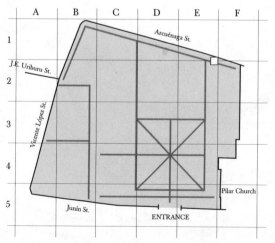

Judge Virgilio Tedín - **E1**

AL JUEZ
Dr VIRGILIO M. TEDÍ
HOMENAJE NACIONAL

Carlos TEJEDOR
Governor of Buenos Aires
1817 - 1903

C arlos Tejedor was a politician who had to undergo exile and political persecution during Rosas' time. He returned to occupy important positions at the Congress House and became, as well, Governor of the Buenos Aires province.

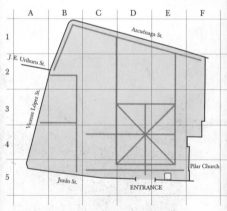

Carlos Tejedor - **E5**

Florencio VARELA
His words were worth a thousand swords
1807 - 1848

W riter, journalist and poet, open oponent to Rosas' regime, he did not stop harassing it from his Montevideo newspapers. He was murdered in Montevideo, apparently after Rosas' order. His family returned to Buenos Aires and his sons continued the family tradition associated with writing and literature. They were related by marriage to Cané, Lainez and Beccar, who also had writers, historians and pressmen among their heirs. His brother, the poet Juan Cruz Varela (1794 – 1839) is buried a few steps away.

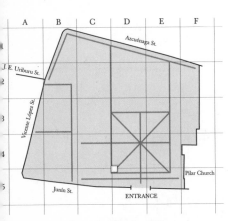

Florencio Varela - D5

Ernesto TORNQUIST

"He ruled the country in the most ample and useful sense of the word..."

1842 - 1908

F amous businessman and banker. His effort and his personal attitude favoured the British mediation to avoid war against Chile at the turning of the 19th century.

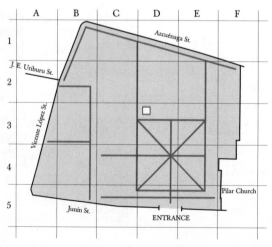

Ernesto Tornquist - D3

José Evaristo URIBURU
Uncle and...
1831 - 1914

P resident of Argentina after Luis Saenz Peña had to give up the government due to lack of political support. He belonged to an ancient family that gave the country more than one statesman.

José Félix URIBURU
Nephew, presidents of the Nation
1868 - 1932

H e was the first General to become President of Argentina after a coup d'état, that drove away Hipólito Yrigoyen from power in 1930.

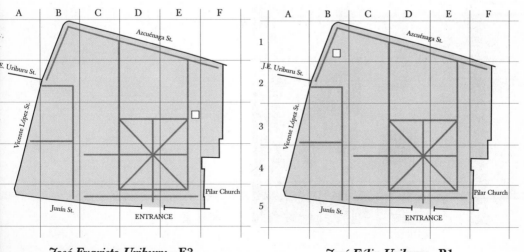

José Evaristo Uriburu - **E3**   *José Félix Uriburu* - **B1**

VERNET
The last Governor of Malvinas Islands
1792 - 1871

He was the first and last Governor of our Islas Malvinas (Falkland Island, as the British call them). Vernet had to stand against the attack of American ships first and English ones later. They took possession of our islands, in spite of all clear facts and data that proved our sovereignty and to the resistance performed by a number of native countrymen led by the "gaucho" Rivero, who was imprisoned by the English but left free by a British judge. He is said to have died fighting against the English and French during the "Vuelta de Obligado" epic battle.

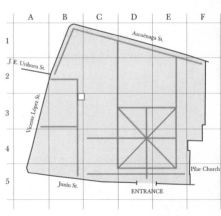

Luis Vernet - **B3**

Alberto WILLIAMS
The musician
1862 - 1952

Williams was one of the most distinghished musicians and educators. He was Amancio Alcorta's grandson, politician and musician as well, from whom Alberto Williams gathered his works. Amancio Williams (1913 – 1989), Alberto's son, was an exquisite architect, disciple of Le Courbousier.

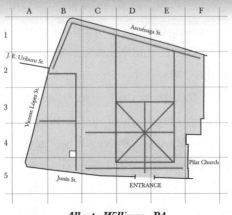

Alberto Williams - B4

CITY OF ANGELS
Walking Itinerary

Once you leave behind the foundation date – 1822 – you will see on the left side, the names of those who participated in the Declaration of Independence, and on the right side the Chris made by Monteverde, the Italian sculptor teacher of Lola Mora.

● Beginning the Red Itinerary ────────────────────

Then face the main street and two parallel corridors.

In case you decide to continue along the main street, see on your right side the monuments of Soler and (P. 111) Brandsen – Independence heroes – and the sculpture (P. 42) of a sleeping girl (daughter of the writer García Velloso). Leftward it raises a huge arch that contains (P. 66) the remains of three generations of the Alvear family: (P. 26) Carlos María (Independence hero and General in the Brazilian War), Torcuato (first Major of Buenos Aires and re-founder of the cemetery) and Marcelo Torcuato de Alvear, President of the Nation and relevant figure of the Radical Party. The design belongs to Christophersen, the same architect that built the Anchorena's elegant mansion, at the present time occupied by the Ministry of Foreign Affairs, just in front of San Martín Square.

QUIROGA

By Alvear's side, stands a statue resembling a virgin, but it is not, since it represents Facundo Quiroga's wife, courageous provincial leader killed in *(P. 100)* an ambush, and who, according to a legend, is buried standing up like the "macho" man he was. The sculpture belongs to Tartadini, and you will notice that it has been reproduced on several tombs.

OCAMPO

If you keep on walking towards the Christ at the centre, you will see two tombs that close the corridors, one is named after Gabriel Ocampo and another after Miguel Belgrano – brother of the General who created our National Flag. These were previous to the reconstruction of the cemetery and were not moved from their original places.

DORREGO

Towards the right, and before reaching the Pantheon of *(P. 54)* Outstanding Citizens, you will find Luis Dorrego's vault, *(P. 58)* where heartless thieves, self called "The Night Chevaliers" took his wife's coffin away, to exchange it for a large ransom. In front of it, leftwards, you will see his brother's vault – Governor Manuel *(P. 59)* Dorrego – where there are always two carnations, one red, another white, as a symbol of the unity of our people after so many years of civil war, that started when he was executed by General Lavalle.

OUTSTANDING CITIZENS

Rightwards, there is a number of simple amphoras were the outstanding citizens are buried. Among them, Saavedra, Perdriel, Sáenz, Estomba, Funes y Peña – with a beautiful sculpture of the Italian Livi. Almost in front of Saavedra and on the aisle, there is an English gravestone that was left there after the 1881 reconstruction. *(P. 54)*

CHRIST

LÓPEZ LECUBE

From Zonza Briano's Christ at the centre, you will enjoy a splendid view of some of the most important monuments of the whole cemetery. To the left (besides Dorrego) López Lecube's *(P. 71)* vault stands with sculptures by Lola Mora. Immediately behind, there is the Jules Coutan's artpiece made for José C. Paz, perhaps *(P. 84)* the most extraordinary sculpture of the entire place. In front of it, you will see Gen. Martín Rodriguez' statue – founder of the *(P. 98)* cemetery – made by Arturo Dresco.

JOSÉ C. PAZ

RODRIGUEZ

RICCHIERI

(P. 104)

Just in front of the Central Christ you can appreciate General Ricchieri's Pantheon, monumental sculpture belonging to Luis Perlotti – that not only keeps the General and his family, but also heroes of San Martín's epic campaigns, such as the Irishman O'Brien, General Quesada and San Martín's conflicting secretary Bernardo Monteagudo, murdered in Peru.

FAHY

Towards Ricchieri's left, crossing the street, there stands the monument with which the Irish community pays homage to Father Fahy. *(P. 64)*

ATUCHA

If you continue clockwise, across the main street, you will reach the mausoleum of the Atucha Lima family crowned by the figure of a woman with her face covered as sign of grief. *(P. 34)*

REMEDIOS DE ESCALADA

Rightwards you will find the Liberator's corner, that kept the remains of his parents – today in Yapeyú, his native town – and those of his beloved wife, Remedios de Escalada. *(P. 57)*

BROWN

GUIDO

(P. 46) **S**tanding across the avenue, a green mast and a crypt, belonged to Admiral Brown and General Guido respectively. Behind them, (P. 68)
(P. 116) Mariquita Sánchez de Mendeville lies and just in front of her place the
(P. 94) mausoleum of Dr. Rawson stands, made in France by Carriere Belleuse.

RAWSON

MENDEVILLE

GRACIARENA

If we keep on walking along this diagonal, leftwards, our eyes will be caught by a group of sculptures made for the Graciarena family by a brilliant but unknown local artist named Víctor Godin. (P. 75)

Some yards ahead, a nameless pyramid – fully masonic work – will catch your attention.

PALACIOS

If you deviate, a little ahead by a corridor towards the left, you will be able to visit the vault of the politician and socialist leader Alfredo Palacios, that bears just humble bronze plaques from few followers and admirers.

DOMINGUITO

CENOTAPH OF THE THREE FRIENDS

Back to the diagonal you will reach a patio "the yard of the lost youth" – that contains the truncated column where Dominguito (P. 118) Sarmiento rests. To his side stands the beautiful winged angel of the "Cenotaph of the Three Friends". A homage to three young artists, close friends between them, who died the same year.

Surrounding it, you can notice the black tomb of the Atuchas and neighbour to it there is a yellow vault that keeps the remains of former President

PIRÁN

LEDESMA

Derqui. Likewise, you will appreciate the angels on the door of what used to be Hoffmann family's vault, and a little frontwards, leaving the patio behind and almost against the Church wall, stands the impeccable chapel of the Guiraldes family. Back again in the patio, you will admire the bust of General Pirán and the angel of Fabián Ledesma (a little behind it, there stands Clodomiro Ledesma's one) both artworks by Biggi. On the left hand side, the vault of the Navy Officer Piedrabuena can be seen and the bust of historian Zinny, just in front of the tomb that belonged to the General and former Police Chief, Rosendo Fraga.

PIEDRABUENA

ZINNY

Start walking along the avenue that leads to far back of the Cemetery, parallel to the main corridor where we started, leave behind the monolith remembering Erasmo Obligado, Navy heroe, and the niche of Pastor Obligado – first Constitutional Governor of Buenos Aires province. Then, it can also be seen, leftwards, the Egyptian style pyramidal tomb of Dr. Arata, physician and chemist.

ARATA

OBLIGADO

ORTIZ DORREGO

Some steps ahead, at the intersection of another avenue there arises the overwhelming vault of the Ortiz Basualdo Dorrego. Walking *(P. 80)* along one of the lateral corridors you will reach an elevated yard, presenting on the right side the low vault belonging to Victorica's, where the General as well as his brother – Colón Theatre decorator – rest. Behind you will be amazed upon the sight of a building of pink granite belonging to the Barthis Soler family, of evident Egyptian style. In a dramatic contrast, just on its side there stands the sober construction in black marble of architect Christophersen. A little forward, you will find two of the most beautiful monuments of the Recoleta, the Massone's vault, which keeps a famous leader and journalist

MASSONE
(P. 74)

GATH

of the Italian community, and just aside the present vault of González Kondrich that belonged to Alfredo Gath, both monuments made by sculptor Bistolfi. *(P. 67)*

VALSECCHI

PASO

(P. 20)

(P. 108)

Back again to the original path, go on walking until you arrive at the intersection with a diagonal where you will meet Alberdi's monument, in a silent discussion with Juan Manuel de Rosas, buried few yards away. In the neighbourhood, you can appreciate the beautiful Valsecchi's door – diplomat and economist – and the tomb of one of the members of our first Patriotic Group, lawyer Juan José Paso. *(P. 81)*

ALBERDI

• Beginning the Blue Itinerary

CAMPOS   ALCORTA

Undoing the way along this diagonal, return to the central Christ and turning rightwards you can see on the left hand side Julio and Gaspar Campos monuments, both dead in civil quarrels. In front of them there stands a sculpture of the *(P. 133)* Alcorta family – politicians and musicians. Go on walking through the main corridor...

PACHECO

On the left hand side you can see Gen. Angel Pacheco's vault, Independence war hero, Rosas's soldier and grandfather of the President Marcelo T. de Alvear.

Rightwards, you will find the ancient tombs of Generals Azcuénaga and Díaz Vélez, both Army leaders and powerful landowners.

PELLEGRINI

In front you will see a low grave with the name Aramburu *(P. 32)* and behind the excellent Pellegrini's sculpture showing him *(P. 86)*

ARAMBURU   as a leader addressing the crowd.

MOSCONI

Surrounding this patio, there are the monuments to Gen. Mosconi – first President of the Fiscal Oil Fields – and Hermes Quijada – Admiral.

OCAMP

Behind, another wide platform guards the remains of writer Victoria Ocampo and her grandfather – Radical Party leader – who was once candidate to the Vice-Presidency of the Nation.

CHASSAING

Just to its right there is a monument rendering homage to a young poet and politician Chassaing, with a statue that despite the fact of being considered National Monument it is in a pretty poor condition.

CAPOZZOLO
CAPRILE

Keep on walking and admire a huge Christ statue that belonged to Capozzolo family and just to its front, the beautiful sculpture of Emma Nicolay de Caprile made by Lucio Morea Corrales, one of our *(P. 23)* most outstanding national sculptors.

ROVERANO
TORNQUIST

If you return to Pellegrini's place, and make a right turn, you *(P. 106)* will find former President, General Roca's tomb. To its right, *(P. 97)* Roverano's vault. Around this yard, enjoy watching the tomb of the musician López Bouchardo crowded with bronze plaques, and a little bit inside the brilliant sculpture for Ernesto Tornquist's tomb, facing a *(P. 128)* granite greeklike building, its door was designed by ROCA Troiano Troiani and belonged to the Peirano family.

In the previous corridor, backwards to Tornquist's monument, the former President Juárez Celman's tomb stands, an old italian like building practically dismantled at the present time. In front of it there is a statue and engravings that renders homage and remembers the brave Colonel César Díaz, who refused the General badge because he didn't gain it at battle.

MARCO DEL PONT

WILDE

Returning to Roca's place, you can walk again along the diagonal that leads to the Central Christ meeting the tombs of Wilde, Santamarina, Olivera and Marco del Pont (politician, landowner, founder of the "Rural" – cattle owners society – and philatelist respectively), or, on the contrary you can continue walking along the avenue up to one of the most visited places of the cemetery – Rufina Cambaceres' tomb. Along the way, *(P. 48)* you can see the strange sculpture belonging to Ignacio De Las Carreras, facing the monument of the philanthropist Méndez Andes.

OLIVERA

SANTAMARINA

CAMBACERES

MENDEZ ANDES

LARROQUE

A little bit inside, neighbouring De Las Carreras, if you look upwards you will appreciate Professor Larroque sitting on a chair.

UNZUÉ

Walking backwards, turn left and towards the Central Christ through the main aisle, you will rejoice with the view of another Christ in the vault of Mariano Unzué and the beautiful angel with trumpet on the top of the Pujol vault. Some steps *(P. 92)* ahead, turn left to see a true masonic tomb, with all its symbolic icons inside. "Obediencia a la Ley". *(P. 72)*

PUJOL

MASONIC TOMB

Arriving at the mythical Rufina's monument, turn right until the next avenue, converted into a full art gallery exhibition. Now, if you go towards the exit, (turn left in this crossroad) don't miss the beautiful sculpture of a mother and her child inside the Orfeli's vault.

● Beginning the Green Itinerary ————————————

PEREYRA YRAOLA   ALZAGA GUERRERO

JACQUES

MITRE

(P. 88)

CROCIATI

Start watching the huge Pereyra Yraola's vault, facing the Alzaga – Guerrero's one. Followed by the tombs *(P. 28)* of Amadeo Jacques and Suárez Laspiur Borges, the place *(P. 120)* that should have occupied Borges and where nowadays the remains of his mother and grandparents rest, the mythical Colonel Suárez – reduced to a small coffin that shares with his friend Colonel Olavarría – as it can be easily seen from the door, as well as the poem his grandson wrote to him.

Then, follow the tombs of Dardo Rocha – founder of La Plata city – Angel Estrada and Peralta Ramos – founder of the newspaper "La Razón" – and then the beautiful monument in homage to former President General Mitre *(P. 76)* and the statue for Marco Avellaneda – the Martyr of Metán *(P. 36)* – that his son (another President) built-up to his memory. In front, you can see the statue of Crociatti and her dog Sabu. *(P. 53)*

ESTRADA

ALVEAR

PERALTA RAMOS

Within this area, you can visit President Sarmiento mausoleum, which he himself designed in a masonic fashion. *(P. 119)*

SARMIENTO

GOMEZ

Just in this crossroad of two avenues, you will be able to watch the sleeping angel in Francisco Gómez' vault, cover of this book.

IDA

(P. 60) Three blocks ahead, turn left, and you will meet this sort of pilgrimage place in which has become Eva Duarte de Perón's tomb. Keep on walking some steps ahead, and you will see the sculpture of a woman lying on the upper part, extending her hand. There are only three letters "IDA". Such was the name of a young lady who died when she fell from a building, and her family rendered their love and respect with this outstanding construction.

EVA DUARTE

DE ANGELIS

PEDRO DE ANGELIS
Fallecido el 10 de Febrero
de 1859
a los 76 años de edad

Y SU ESPOSA
MELANIE DAVET
DE ANGELIS
Fallecida el 2 de Noviembre
de 1879
a los 89 años de edad

Again, back along in the main street you can watch the plaque that remembers the learned historian Pedro de Angelis, just by the old tomb of Vernet, last Governor of the Malvinas Islands.

OTAMENDI

If you turn left, one block before the last street, rejoice at the sight of the monumental Otamendi's vault with an extraordinary angel inside, just by the gothic temple that Mrs. Noel de Ramos Otero built in memory of her husband.

Nearby, Dr. Agote's tomb, the first physician to perform a blood transfusion. Looking upwards, watch the beautiful statue of Juncosa Seré – surely in loving memory of a dead child. A little ahead, General Day built his sculpture standing-up, guarding his own tomb.

LELOIR

Back again to the main avenue, we approach to its end and then turning a little bit right, you can see in front of you the beautiful bronze angel of the Estrougamou family, and appreciate at your right a little far ahead one of the tallest tombs of the cemetery, the one of the Nobel Prize winner Federico Leloir –.

MITRE   AVELLANEDA

Please turn left and keep on walking up to the end. Here you will appreciate a number of various tombs: (first Emilio Mitre's – engineer and Director of "La Nación" newspaper). Then Nicolás Avellaneda – President of the *(P. 36)* Nation. Ahead there are the General brothers' tombs, Luis María Campos and Manuel Campos. *(P. 50)*

L. CAMPOS   M. CAMPOS

VIEJOBUENO   MORRA

Rightwards, you can see the sober tomb of Costaguta. Following leftwards, neighbour to the boundaries of the *(P. 112)* cemetery, Roque Sáenz Peña – President of the Nation, Carlos *(P. 78)* Morra – architect –, Devoto – businessman – and the *(P. 56)* Pantheon of Paraguayan Warriors – *(P. 82)* DEVOTO guarded by two bronze soldiers.

SÁENZ PEÑA

PANTHEON OF
PARAGUAY WARRIORS

VASENA   COSTAGUTTÁ

In front you can watch the angels that guard the General Viejobueno, and the Vasena vault with an angel of death, gazing through his hood.

FALCÓN

LARTIGAU

Finally, reach the corner where the Lartigau and Colonel Falcón monuments stand, both murdered near the cemetery *(P. 62)* in an anarchist coup at the beginning of the 20th century.

OLIVERA

From here, you walk along the avenue that runs parallel to the wall on Azcuénaga street. You can see the extraordinary artwork done by sculptor *(P. 79)* Lucio Fontana for Cisnetto Olivera – real masterpiece of matchless value. Afterwards, a beautiful angel crowns the entrance of the Mattaldi's vault.

LONARDI

AYERZA

QUINTANA

Following this path, you will see the tombs of Rodríguez Achával (politician), Ricardo Gutiérrez (doctor and poet), Quintana – (President of the Nation) –, Norberto de la Riestra *(P. 96)*

RODRIGUEZ ACHAVAL

FIRPO

(economist), Firpo – (famous box fighter – *(P. 65)* sculpture made by Luis Perlotti), the Pantheon of the Polish Community, the modern structure of Noble's tomb (newspaperman).

ELIZALDE

Towards the right, Menéndez, Martín Coronado, Gelly y Obes, *(P. 40)* Pierre Benoit and nearby José Hernández, author of "Martín Fierro". Rufino Elizalde by sculptor Riganelli, Pantheon of the 1890 Revolution, where famous *(P. 102)*

MENÉNDEZ BEHETY

DE LA RIESTRA

leaders and Presidents of the Radical Party lie (Irigoyen, Illia, Alem, etc); the statue of Dr. *(P. 38)* Ayerza until we meet the monument of Del Carril family. We *(P. 52)* will see here the descending cross by Rovati on the tomb that nowadays keeps the remains of General Lonardi and the *(P. 70)* beautiful artwork of Sansebastino for Judge Tedín. *(P. 124)*

DEL CARRIL

1890 REVOLUTION

POLISH COMMUNITY

Gral. de Brig. Bronislaw RAKOW
20.6.1895 - 25.12.1950
Gral. de Brig. Jan ŚWIERCZEŃSKI V. M.
5.1.1897 - 19.1.1969
Gral. de Brig. Jerzy Aleksander ZAWISZA V. M.
18.6.1895 - 23.2.1995

GELLY

LÓPEZ

LAVALLE

(P. 69) **T**hen comes Lavalle's tomb and his grenadier (that keeps a resemblance to the General himself) who is guarding his sleep and the Cenotaph of Lucio Vicente López – grandson of the author of our National Anthem – made by the French sculptor Falguiere.

QUESADA

DEL VALLE

Inside dark vaults, find Aristóbulo del Valle and General Isidro Quesada.

ALSINA

ALCORTA

Rightwards, meet the monumental work to Adolfo Alsina and *(P. 24)* facing it the sculpture of President Figueroa Alcorta with three women representing the three powers he performed (legislative, executive and judicial), the bust was made by Fioravanti.

BULLRICH

Turning our sight you will see the vault of Brown Hale – American businessman friend of Sarmiento's. Some yards behind, there are plaques remembering Adolfo Bullrich – a progressive Major of Buenos Aires.

GONÇÁLVEZ BORREGA   LEGUIZAMÓN

We start our return itinerary along the avenue that leads us up to the Alberdi's monument, passing along the mausoleum of Gonçálvez Borrega and the curious tomb of the *(P. 75)* writer, historian and numismatist Martiniano Leguizamón, that reproduces itself.

AVELLANEDA
HERLIZTKA

On the left, one of the few French tombs and the byzantin construction of the Herliztka's vault. If you make a left, enjoy with the view of the beautiful door *(P. 34)* of the Sarassa Atucha, the semicircle of Marco Avellaneda (Jr) made by Cardona and the glass vault that allows us to see the coffin of the sportsman Charly Menditegui.

MENDITEGUI

OSSORIO ARANA

Go back to the avenue and walk along again by Alberdi, Ortiz Basualdo and Dominguito to meet the first street parallel to Junín. If you turn right you will find a statue of Fioravanti made for Gen. Ossorio Arana.

ANDRADE

On the left hand side, we find the Ezcurra family tomb – it keeps the remains of Josefa Ezcurra, Belgrano's lover – and also the poet Olegario Andrade – where Ramón Lista is also buried, his son-in-law, first Governor of a Patagonian province.

RODRÍGUEZ PEÑA

Towards the left, almost reaching the main entrance, there stands the National Monument honouring Rodríguez Peña (member of our first National Government 1810).

MAYER BROTHERS

When we reach again the first patio behind Garcia Velloso's tomb and the Soldier's statue, there is a green small temple – where the Mayer brothers rest: Carlos, dead at the early age of 20 and Edelmiro, who was General not only of the Argentinian, but also of the American and Mexican army, and, likewise, Governor of Chubut province.

ANCHORENA

LEZICA

GALLARDO

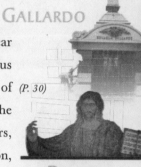

Keep walking until you leave behind the Alvear
Arch; you will see Esnaola Gallardo, the tumulus
of the first of the Anchorenas', the sober tomb of *(P. 30)*
Faustino Lezica and the painter Beristayn, where the
writer Leopoldo Lugones was buried during 50 years,
and further Juan Pueyrredón monument which was made by his son,
the artist Prilidiano Pueyrredón. *(P. 90)*

BERISTAYN

F. VARELA

MARTINEZ DE HOZ

Turn right, along that street and you will meet
Pedro Anchorena, Rómulo Naón and the
patio with the central monument of Valentín *(P. 24)*
Alsina, surrounded by Casares, Martínez de Hoz
(horse breaders and governors), writer Agustín
(P. 89) Alvarez, Ramos Mejía, Florencio Varela – murdered
in Montevideo – as it is written in his coffin; some
yards ahead his brother rests, the poet Juan
Cruz Varela.

ALSINA

J. C. VARELA

ALVAREZ

ANCHORE

VELAZ

Follow our return itinerary, and walk along the diagonal that leads to
the Main Christ, then pass along the monument in honour of Velaz. If
we keep on walking along the little street neighbour to Ramos Mejía, you
will finish in a dead-end street, leaving behind Adolfo Carranza – historian –,
Virasoro – Governor of Corrientes province –, and finally a gorgeous door
reproducing Christ's Passion.

BRIANO'S CHRIST

This is how we reach the Christ figure, sober artwork of Zonza Briano, that shows this Just and Severe God, Judge to our sins.

We leave the Recoleta Cemetery overwhelmed by our ancient history and the magnificent artworks that are treasured here, patrimony of our nation and of the world as well.

INDEX

INDEX

ITINERARY

SURNAME & NAME	OCCUPATION	COOR.	ITINERARY
MITRE	President	B4	Green
MORRA, Carlos	Architect	B1	Green
OLIVERA CISNETTO	Landowner	C1	Green
ORTIZ BASUALDO	Landowner	E4	Red
PASO, Juan José	Politician	E3	Red / Green
Pantheon of Paraguayan Warriors	Pantheon	B1	Green
PAZ, José Camilo	Newspaperman	D4	Blue
PELLEGRINI, Carlos	President	D3	Blue
PERALTA RAMOS, Patricio	Newspaperman	B4	Green
RAMOS MEJIA	Physician	D4	Green
PUEYRREDON, Juan Martín de	Soldier	C5	Green
PUEYRREDON, Prilidiano	Painter	C5	Green
PUJOL, Juan	Politician	C4	Blue
RAWSON, William Collisbery	Physician	D4	Red
QUINTANA, Manuel	President	D1	Green
ROVERANO	Merchant	C3	Blue
RODRIGUEZ, Martín	Soldier - Founder of Recoleta	D4	Blue
QUIROGA, Juan Facundo	Soldier - Politician	D5	Green / Red
1890 Revolution	Pantheon	E1	Green
RICCHIERI, Pablo	Soldier	D4	Blue / Red
ROCA, Julio Argentino	President	D3	Blue
ROSAS, Juan Manuel de	Soldier - Politician	E3	Red / Green
SAAVEDRA LAMAS, Carlos	Nobel Prize Winner	F3	Red
SOLER, Miguel Estanislao	Soldier	D5	Green / Red
SAENZ PEÑA, Luis	President	D5	Green
SAENZ PEÑA, Roque	President	B2	Green
SAENZ VALIENTE, Casto	Landowner	D2	Blue
SANCHEZ de THOMPSON, Mariquita	Civic Leader	E4	Red
SARMIENTO, Domingo Fidel	Soldier	E5	Red / Green
SARMIENTO, Domingo Faustino	President	B4	Green
SUAREZ, Isidro	Soldier	B4	Green
SPINETTO	Businessman	B3	Green
TEDIN, Virgilio	Judge	E1	Green
TEJEDOR, Carlos	Politician	E5	Green
VARELA, Florencio	Newspaperman	D5	Green
TORNQUIST, Ernesto	Businessman	D3	Blue
URIBURU, José Evaristo	Politician	E3	Green
URIBURU, José Félix	President	B1	Green
VERNET, Luis	Politician	B3	Green
WILLIAMS, Alberto	Musician	B4	Green

SURNAME & NAME	OCCUPATION	COOR.	ITINERARY
ALBERDI, Juan Bautista	Lawyer	E3	Red / Green
ALLENO, David	Warden of the Recoleta	C2	Green
CAPRILE, Emma Nicolay de	Teacher	E2	Blue
ALSINA, Valentín	Politician	C5	Green
ALSINA, Adolfo	Politician	E1	Green
ALVEAR, Marcelo T. de	President	D5	Red / Green
ALVEAR, Diego de	Landowner	C4	Blue
ALZAGA	Businessman	B5	Green
ANCHORENA	Landowner	B3 / C5 / D5	Green
ARAMBURU, Pedro Eugenio	Lawyer	D3	Blue
ATUCHA	Landowner	D4 / E5 / F2	Red / Green
AVELLANEDA	Politician's Family	B2 / B4 / F3	Red / Green
AYERZA, José Toribio	Physician	E1	Green
BENOIT, Pierre	Architect	C1	Green
BRANDSEN, Federico	Soldier	D5	Red / Green
BRITISH TOMBS	Tombs	D4 / E5	Blue / Red / Green
BROWN, William	Navy Heroe	D4	Red
CAMBACERES, Rufina	Lady in white	C4	Blue
CAMPOS, Luis María	Soldier	B2	Green
CAMPOS, Manuel	Soldier	B1	Green
DEL CARRIL, Bonifacio	Vice-President	E1	Green
CROCIATTI	Landowner	B4	Green
Pantheon of Outstanding Citizens	Pantheon	D4	Red
DEVOTO	Businessman	B1	Green
ESCALADA, Remedios de	San Martin's wife	D4	Red
DORREGO, Luis	Businessman	D4	Red / Green
DORREGO, Manuel	Soldier	D4	Red / Green
DUARTE DE PERON, Eva	Landowner	B3	Green
FALCON, Ramón and LARTIGAU, Juan	Policemen	B1	Green
FAHY, Antonio	Priest	D4	Blue
FIRPO, Luis Angel	Boxer	D1	Green
GARCIA VELLOSO, Luz María	Writer	D5	Red / Green
GATH, Alfred	Businessman	F3	Red / Green
GUIDO, Tomás	Soldier	E4	Red
LAVALLE, Juan Galo	Soldier	E1	Green
LONARDI	President	E1	Green
LOPEZ LECUBE, Ramón	Landowner	D4	Red / Green / Blue
MASONIC TOMBS	Tombs	D2 / D4 / E4	Green/Blue/Red
MASSONE	Businessman	F4	Red
MAUSOLEUM	Tombs	D4 / E2	Red / Green

This book was printed and bound in
Gráfica Integral S.A., Buenos Aires, Argentina.
May 2002.